PUBLIC POWER IN THE AGE OF EMPIRE

PUBLIC POWER
IN THE AGE OF EMPIRE

ARUNDHATI ROY

Open Media Pamphlet Series

SEVEN STORIES PRESS / NEW YORK

Seven Stories Press
140 Watts Street
New York, NY 10013
www.sevenstories.com

In Canada:
Publishers Group Canada, 250A Carlton Street, Toronto, ON M5A-2L1

Library of Congress Cataloging-in-Publication Data

Roy, Arundhati.
  Public power in the age of empire / Arundhati Roy.-- A Seven Stories
Press 1st ed.
    p. cm.
  ISBN 1-58322-682-6 (pbk. : alk. paper)
  1. Government, Resistance to. 2. Power (Social sciences) 3.
Imperialism. 4. Terrorism--India--Prevention. 5. War on Terrorism,
2001- I. Title.
JC328.3.R68 2004
320.954'01'1--dc22

                                        2004021833

College professors may order examination copies of
Seven Stories Press titles for a free six-month trial period.
To order, visit www.sevenstories.com/textbook, or fax on
school letterhead to (212) 226-1411.

Book design by: Jon Gilbert

9 8 7 6 5 4 3 2 1

Printed in Canada.

When language has been butchered and bled of meaning, how do we understand "public power"? When freedom means occupation, when democracy means neoliberal capitalism, when reform means repression, when words like "empowerment" and "peacekeeping" make your blood run cold—why, then, "public power" could mean whatever you want it to mean. A biceps building machine, or a Community Power Shower. So, I'll just have to define "public power" as I go along, in my own self-serving sort of way.

In India, the word *public* is now a Hindi word. It means *people*. In Hindi, we have *sarkar* and *public*, the government and the people. Inherent in this use is the underlying assumption that the government is quite separate from "the people." This distinction has to do with the fact that India's freedom struggle, though magnificent, was by no means revolutionary. The Indian elite stepped easily and elegantly into the shoes of the British imperialists. A deeply impoverished, essentially feudal society became a modern, independent nation state. Even today, fifty-seven years on to the day, the truly vanquished still look upon the government as *mai-baap*, the parent and provider. The somewhat more radical, those who still have fire in their bellies, see it as *chor*, the thief, the snatcher-away of all things.

Either way, for most Indians, *sarkar* is very separate from *public*. However, as you make your way up India's complex social ladder, the distinction between *sarkar* and *public* gets blurred. The Indian elite, like the elite anywhere in the world, finds it hard to separate itself from the state. It sees like the state, thinks like the state, speaks like the state.

In the United States, on the other hand, the blurring of the distinction between *sarkar* and *public* has penetrated far deeper into society. This could be a sign of a robust democracy, but unfortunately, it's a little more complicated and less pretty than that. Among other things, it has to do with the elaborate web of paranoia generated by the U.S. *sarkar* and spun out by the corporate media and Hollywood. Ordinary people in the United States have been manipulated into imagining they are a people under siege whose sole refuge and protector is their government. If it isn't the Communists, it's al-Qaeda. If it isn't Cuba, it's Nicaragua. As a result, this, the most powerful nation in the world—with its unmatchable arsenal of weapons, its history of having waged and sponsored endless wars, and the only nation in history to have actually used nuclear

7

bombs—is peopled by a terrified citizenry, jumping at shadows. A people bonded to the state not by social services, or public health care, or employment guarantees, but by fear.

This synthetically manufactured fear is used to gain public sanction for further acts of aggression. And so it goes, building into a spiral of self-fulfilling hysteria, now formally calibrated by the U.S government's Amazing Technicolored Terror Alerts: fuchsia, turquoise, salmon pink.

To outside observers, this merging of *sarkar* and *public* in the United States sometimes makes it hard to separate the actions of the government from the people. It is this confusion that fuels anti-Americanism in the world. Anti-Americanism is then seized upon and amplified by the U.S. government and its faithful media outlets. You know the routine: "Why do they hate us? They hate our freedoms," et cetera. This enhances the sense of isolation among people in the United States and makes the embrace between *sarkar* and *public* even more intimate. Like Red Riding Hood looking for a cuddle in the wolf's bed.

Two thousand and one was not the first year that the U.S. government declared a "war on terrorism." As Noam Chomsky reminds us, the first "war on terrorism" was declared by President Ronald Reagan in the 1980s during the U.S.-sponsored terrorist wars across Central America, the Middle East, and Africa. The Reagan administration called terrorism a "plague spread by depraved opponents of civilization itself." In keeping with this sentiment, in 1987, the United Nations General Assembly proposed a strongly worded condemnation of terrorism. One hundred and fifty-three countries voted for it. Only the United States and Israel voted against it. They objected to a passage that referred to "the right to self-determination, freedom, and independence . . . of people forcibly deprived of that right . . . particularly peoples under colonial and racist regimes and foreign occupation." Remember that in 1987, the United States was a staunch ally of apartheid South Africa. The African National Congress and Nelson Mandela were listed as "terrorists." The term "foreign occupation" was taken to mean Israel's occupation of Palestine.

Over the last few years, the "war on terrorism" has mutated into the more generic "war on terror." Using the threat of an external enemy to rally people behind you is a tired old horse that politicians have ridden into power for centuries. But could it be that ordinary people are fed up with that poor old horse and are looking for something different? There's an old Hindi film song that goes *yeh public hai, yeh sab jaanti hai* (the public, she knows it all). Wouldn't it be lovely if the song were right and the politicians wrong?

Before Washington's illegal invasion of Iraq, a Gallup International poll showed that in no European country was the support for a unilateral war higher than 11 percent. On February 15, 2003, weeks before the invasion, more than ten million people marched against the war on different continents, including North America. And yet the governments of many supposedly democratic countries still went to war.

The question is: is "democracy" still democratic? Are democratic governments accountable to the people who elected them? And, critically, is the *public* in democratic countries responsible for the actions of its *sarkar?*

If you think about it, the logic that underlies the war on terrorism and the logic that underlies terrorism are exactly the same. Both make ordinary citizens pay for the actions of their government. Al-Qaeda made the people of the United States pay with their lives for the actions of their government in Palestine, Saudi Arabia, Iraq, and Afghanistan. The U.S. government has made the people of Afghanistan pay in the thousands for the actions of the Taliban and the people of Iraq pay in the hundreds of thousands for the actions of Saddam Hussein.

The crucial difference is that nobody really elected al-Qaeda, the Taliban, or Saddam Hussein. But the president of the United States was elected (well . . . in a manner of speaking). The prime ministers of Italy, Spain, and the United Kingdom were elected. Could it then be argued that citizens of these countries are more responsible for the actions of their government than Iraqis were for the actions of Saddam Hussein or Afghans for the Taliban?

Whose God decides which is a "just war" and which isn't? George Bush senior once said: "I will never apologize for the United States. I don't care what the facts are." When the president of the most powerful country in the world doesn't *need* to care what the facts are, then we can at least be sure we have entered the Age of Empire.

So what does public power mean in the Age of Empire? Does it mean anything at all? Does it actually *exist*?

In these allegedly democratic times, conventional political thought holds that public power is exercised through the ballot. Scores of countries in the world will go to the polls this year. Most (not all) of them will get the governments they vote for. But will they get the governments they want?

In India this year, we voted the Hindu nationalists out of office. But even as we celebrated, we knew that on nuclear bombs, neoliberalism, privatization, censorship, big dams—on every major issue other than overt Hindu nationalism—the Congress and the BJP have no major ideological differences. We know that it is the fifty-year legacy of the Congress Party that prepared the ground culturally and politically for the far right. It was also the Congress Party that first opened India's markets to corporate globalization. It passed legislation that encouraged the privatization of water and power, the dismantling of the public sector, and the denationalization of public companies. It enforced cutbacks in government

13

spending on education and health, and weakened labor laws that protected workers' rights. The BJP took this process forward with pitiless abandon.

In its election campaign, the Congress Party indicated that it was prepared to rethink some of its earlier economic policies. Millions of India's poorest people came out in strength to vote in the elections. The spectacle of the great Indian democracy was telecast live—the poor farmers, the old and infirm, the veiled women with their beautiful silver jewelry, making quaint journeys to election booths on elephants and camels and bullock carts. Contrary to the predictions of all India's experts and pollsters, Congress won more votes than any other party. India's communist parties won the largest share of the vote in their history. India's poor had clearly voted against neoliberalism's economic "reforms" and growing fascism. As soon as the votes were counted, the corporate media dispatched them like badly paid extras on a film set. Television channels featured split screens. Half the screen showed the chaos outside the home of Sonia Gandhi, the leader of the Congress Party, as the coalition government was cobbled together. The other half showed frenzied stockbrokers outside the Bombay Stock Exchange, panicking at the thought that the Congress Party might actually honor its promises and implement its electoral mandate. We saw the Sensex stock index move up and down and sideways. The media, whose own publicly listed stocks were plummeting, reported the stock market crash as though Pakistan had launched ICBMs on New Delhi.

Even before the new government was formally sworn in, senior Congress politicians made public statements reassuring investors and the media that privatization of public utilities would continue. Meanwhile the BJP, now in opposition, has cynically, and comically, begun to oppose foreign direct investment and the further opening of Indian markets.

This is the spurious, evolving dialectic of electoral democracy.

As for the Indian poor, once they've provided the votes, they are expected to bugger off home. Policy will be decided despite them.

✧   ✧   ✧

And what of the U.S. elections? Do U.S. voters have a real choice?

It's true that if John Kerry becomes president, some of the oil tycoons and Christian fundamentalists in the White House will change. Few will be sorry to see the backs of Dick Cheney or Donald Rumsfeld or John Ashcroft or an end to their blatant thuggery. But the real concern is that in the new administration their policies will continue. That we will have Bushism without Bush.

Those positions of real power—the bankers, the CEOs—are not vulnerable to the vote (and in any case, they fund both sides).

Unfortunately, U.S. elections have deteriorated into a sort of personality contest, a squabble over who would do a better job of overseeing empire. John Kerry believes in the idea of empire as fervently as George Bush does. The U.S. political system has been carefully crafted to ensure that no one who questions the natural goodness of the military-industrial-corporate structure will be allowed through the portals of power.

Given this, it's no surprise that in this election you have two Yale University graduates, both members of Skull and Bones, the same secret society, both millionaires, both playing at soldier-soldier, both talking up war, and arguing almost childishly about who will lead the war on terror more effectively.

Like President Bill Clinton before him, Kerry will continue the expansion of U.S. economic and military penetration into the world. He says he would have voted to authorize Bush to go to war in Iraq even if he had known that Iraq had no weapons of mass destruction. He promises to commit more troops to Iraq. He said recently that he supports Bush's policies toward Israel and Ariel Sharon "completely." He says he'll retain 98 percent of Bush's tax cuts.

So, underneath the shrill exchange of insults, there is almost absolute consensus. It looks as though even if people in the United States vote for Kerry, they'll still get Bush. President John Kerbush or President George Berry. It's not a real choice. It's an *apparent* choice. Like choosing a brand of detergent. Whether you buy Ivory Snow or Tide, they're both owned by Proctor & Gamble.

This doesn't mean that one takes a position that is without nuance, that the Congress and the BJP, New Labor and the Tories, the Democrats and Republicans are the same. Of course, they're not.

Neither are Tide and Ivory Snow. Tide has oxy-boosting and Ivory Snow is a gentle cleanser.

In India, there is a difference between an overtly fascist party (the BJP) and a party that slyly pits one community against another (Congress), and sows the seeds of communalism that are then so ably harvested by the BJP. There are differences in the I.Q.s and levels of ruthlessness between this year's U.S. presidential candidates. The anti-war movement in the United States has done a phenomenal job of exposing the lies and venality that led to the invasion of Iraq, despite the propaganda and intimidation it faced. This was a service not just to people here, but to the whole world.

But why is it that the Democrats do not even have to pretend to be against the invasion and occupation of Iraq? If the anti-war movement openly campaigns for Kerry, the rest of the world will think that it approves of his policies of "sensitive" imperialism. Is U.S. imperialism preferable if it is supported by the United Nations and European countries? Is it preferable if the UN asks Indian and Pakistani soldiers to do the killing and dying in Iraq instead of U.S. soldiers? Is the only change that Iraqis can hope for that French, German, and Russian companies will share in the spoils of the occupation of their country?

Is this actually better or worse for those of us who live in subject nations? Is it better for the world to have a smarter emperor in power or a stupider one? Is that our only choice?

I'm sorry, I know that these are uncomfortable, even brutal questions, but they must be asked.

The fact is that electoral democracy has become a process of cynical manipulation. It offers us a very reduced political space today. To believe that this space constitutes real choice would be naïve.

The crisis in modern democracy is a profound one. Free elections, a free press, and an independent judiciary mean little when the free market has reduced them to commodities available on sale to the highest bidder.

On the global stage, beyond the jurisdiction of sovereign governments, international instruments of trade and finance oversee a complex web of multilateral laws and agreements that have entrenched a system of appropriation that puts colonialism to shame. This system allows the unrestricted entry and exit of massive amounts of speculative capital—hot money—into and out of third world countries, which then effectively dictates their economic policy. Using the threat of capital flight as a lever, international capital insinuates itself deeper and deeper into these economies. Giant transnational corporations are taking control of their essential infrastructure and natural resources, their minerals, their water, their electricity. The World Trade Organization, the World Bank, the International Monetary Fund, and other financial institutions like the Asian Development Bank, virtually write economic policy and parliamentary legislation. With a deadly combination of arrogance and ruthlessness, they take their sledgehammers to fragile, interdependent, historically complex societies, and devastate them.

All this goes under the fluttering banner of "reform." As a consequence of this reform, in Africa, Asia, and Latin America, thousands of small enterprises and industries have closed down, millions of workers and farmers have lost their jobs and land. Anyone who criticizes this process is mocked for being "anti-reform," anti-progress, anti-development. Somehow a Luddite.

The *Spectator* newspaper in London assures us that "[w]e live in the happiest, healthiest and most peaceful era in human history."

Billions wonder: who's "we"? Where does he live? What's his Christian name?

Once the economies of third world countries are controlled by the free market, they are enmeshed in an elaborate, carefully calibrated system of economic inequality. For example, Western countries that together spend more than one billion dollars a *day* on subsidies to farmers demand that poor countries withdraw all agricultural subsidies, including subsidized electricity. Then they flood the markets of poor countries with their subsidized agricultural goods and other products with which local producers cannot possibly compete.

Countries that have been plundered by colonizing regimes are steeped in debt to these same powers, and have to repay them at the rate of about 382 *billion* dollars a year. Ergo, the rich get richer and the poor get poorer—not accidentally, but by *design*. By *intention*.

To put a vulgar point on all of this—the truth is getting more vulgar by the minute—the combined wealth of the world's billionaires in 2004 (587 "individuals and family units"), according to *Forbes* magazine, is 1.9 trillion dollars. This is more than the gross domestic product of the world's 135 poorest countries combined. The good news is that there are 111 more billionaires this year than there were in 2003. Isn't that fun?

The thing to understand is that modern democracy is safely premised on an almost religious acceptance of the nation state. But corporate globalization is not. Liquid capital is not. So, even though capital needs the coercive powers of the nation state to put down revolts in the servants' quarters, this setup ensures that no individual nation can oppose corporate globalization on its own.

Time and again we have seen the heroes of our times, giants in opposition, suddenly diminished. President Lula of Brazil was the hero of the World Social Forum in January 2002. Now he's busy implementing IMF guidelines, reducing pension benefits and purging radicals from the Workers' Party. Lula has a worthy predecessor in the former president of South Africa, Nelson Mandela, who instituted a massive program of privatization and structural adjustment that has left thousands of people homeless, jobless, and without water and electricity. When Harry Oppenheimer died in August 2000, Mandela called him "one of the great South Africans of our time." Oppenheimer was the head of Anglo-American, one of South Africa's largest mining companies, which made its money exploiting cheap black labor made available by the repressive apartheid regime.

Why does this happen? It is neither true nor useful to dismiss Mandela or Lula as weak or treacherous people. It's important to understand the nature of the beast they were up against. The moment they crossed the floor from the opposition into government they became hostage to a spectrum of threats—most malevolent among them the threat of capital flight, which can destroy any government overnight. To imagine that a leader's personal charisma and history of struggle will dent the corporate cartel is to have no understanding of how capitalism works, or for that matter, how power works.

Radical change cannot and will not be negotiated by governments; it can only be enforced by people. By the *public*. A public who can link hands *across* national borders.

So when we speak of public power in the age of Empire, I hope it's not presumptuous to assume that the only thing that is worth discussing seriously is the power of a *dissenting* public. A public that *disagrees* with the very concept of empire. A public that has set itself against incumbent power—international, national, regional, or provincial governments and institutions that support and service Empire.

Of course those of us who live in Empire's subject nations are aware that in the great cities of Europe and the United States, where a few years ago these things would only have been whispered, there is now open talk about the benefits of imperialism and the need for a strong empire to police an unruly world. It wasn't long ago that colonialism also sanctified itself as a "civilizing mission." So we can't give these pundits high marks for originality.

We are aware that New Imperialism is being marketed as a "lesser evil" in a less-than-perfect world. Occasionally some of us are invited to "debate" the merits of imperialism on "neutral" platforms provided by the corporate media. It's like debating slavery. It isn't a subject that deserves the dignity of a debate.

What are the avenues of protest available to people who wish to resist empire? By resist I don't mean only to *express* dissent, but to effectively force change.

Empire has a range of calling cards. It uses different weapons to break open different markets. There isn't a country on God's earth that is not caught in the cross hairs of the U.S. cruise missile and the IMF checkbook. Argentina's the model if you want to be the poster boy of neoliberal capitalism, Iraq if you're the black sheep.

For poor people in many countries, Empire does not always appear in the form of cruise missiles and tanks, as it has in Iraq or Afghanistan or Vietnam. It appears in their lives in very local avatars—losing their jobs, being sent unpayable electricity bills, having their water supply cut, being evicted from their homes and uprooted from their land. All this overseen by the repressive machinery of the state, the police, the army, the judiciary. It is a process of relentless impoverishment with which the poor are historically familiar. What Empire does is to further entrench and exacerbate already existing inequalities.

Even until quite recently, it was sometimes difficult for people to see themselves as victims of Empire. But now local struggles have begun to see their role with increasing clarity. However grand it might sound, the fact is, they *are* confronting Empire in their own, very different ways. Differently in Iraq, in South Africa, in India, in Argentina, and differently, for that matter, on the streets of Europe and the United States.

Mass resistance movements, individual activists, journalists, artists, and film makers have come together to strip Empire of its sheen. They have connected the dots, turned cash-flow charts and boardroom speeches into real stories about real people and real despair. They have shown how the neoliberal project has cost people their homes, their land, their jobs, their liberty, their dignity. They have made the intangible tangible. The once seemingly incorporeal enemy is now corporeal.

This is a huge victory. It was forged by the coming together of disparate political groups, with a variety of strategies. But they all recognized that the target of their anger, their activism, and their doggedness is the same. This was the beginning of *real* globalization. The globalization of dissent.

Broadly speaking, there are two kinds of mass resistance movements in third world countries today.

The landless people's movement in Brazil, the anti-dam movement in India, the Zapatistas in Mexico, the Anti-Privatization Forum in South Africa, and hundreds of others, are fighting their own sovereign governments, which have become agents of the neoliberal project. Most of these are radical struggles, fighting to change the structure and chosen model of "development" of their own societies.

Then there are those fighting formal and brutal neocolonial occupations in contested territories whose boundaries and fault lines were often arbitrarily drawn last century by the imperialist powers. In Palestine, Tibet, Chechnya, Kashmir, and several states in India's northeast provinces, people are waging struggles for self-determination.

Several of these struggles might have been radical, even revolutionary when they began, but often the brutality of the repression they face pushes them into conservative, even retrogressive spaces where they use the same violent strategies and the same language of religious and cultural nationalism used by the states they seek to replace.

Many of the foot soldiers in these struggles will find, like those who fought apartheid in South Africa, that once they overcome overt occupation, they will be left with another battle on their hands—a battle against covert economic colonialism.

Meanwhile, the rift between rich and poor is being driven deeper and the battle to control the world's resources intensifies. Economic colonialism through formal military aggression is staging a comeback.

Iraq today is a tragic illustration of this process. An illegal invasion. A brutal occupation in the name of liberation. The rewriting of laws that allow the shameless appropriation of the country's wealth and resources by corporations allied to the occupation, and now the charade of a local "Iraqi government."

For these reasons, it is absurd to condemn the resistance to the U.S. occupation in Iraq as being

masterminded by terrorists or insurgents or supporters of Saddam Hussein. After all, if the United States
were invaded and occupied, would everybody who
fought to liberate it be a terrorist or an insurgent or
a Bushite?

The Iraqi resistance is fighting on the frontlines
of the battle against Empire. And therefore that battle is our battle.

Like most resistance movements, it combines a
motley range of assorted factions. Former Baathists,
liberals, Islamists, fed-up collaborationists, communists, etc. Of course, it is riddled with opportunism,
local rivalry, demagoguery, and criminality. But if
we are only going to support pristine movements,
then no resistance will be worthy of our purity.

A whole industry of development experts, aca-
demics, and consultants have built an industry on
the back of global social movements in which they
are not direct participants. Many of these "experts,"
who earn their livings studying the struggles of the

world's poor, are funded by groups like the Ford Foundation, the World Bank, and wealthy universities such Harvard, Stanford, and Cornell. From a safe distance, they offer us their insightful critiques. But the same people who tell us that we can reform the World Bank from within, that we change the IMF by working inside it, would not themselves seek to reform a resistance movement by working within it.

This is not to say that we should never criticize resistance movements. Many of them suffer from a lack of democracy, from the iconization of their "leaders," a lack of transparency, a lack of vision and direction. But most of all they suffer from vilification, repression, and lack of resources.

Before we prescribe how a pristine Iraqi resistance must conduct a secular, feminist, democratic, nonviolent battle, we should shore up our end of the resistance by forcing the U.S. government and its allies to withdraw from Iraq.

❖ ❖ ❖

The first militant confrontation in the United States between the global justice movement and the neoliberal junta took place famously at the WTO conference in Seattle in December 1999. To many mass movements in developing countries that had long been fighting lonely, isolated battles, Seattle was the first delightful sign that their anger and their vision of another kind of world was shared by people in the imperialist countries.

In January 2001, in Porto Alegre, Brazil, 20,000 activists, students, film makers—some of the best minds in the world—came together to share their experiences and exchange ideas about confronting Empire. That was the birth of the now historic World Social Forum. It was the first formal coming together of an exciting, anarchic, unindoctrinated, energetic, new kind of "public power." The rallying cry of the

WSF is "Another World is Possible." The forum has become a platform where hundreds of conversations, debates, and seminars have helped to hone and refine a vision of what kind of world it should be. By January 2004, when the fourth WSF was held in Mumbai, India, it attracted 200,000 delegates. I have never been part of a more electrifying gathering. It was a sign of the social forum's success that the mainstream media in India ignored it completely. But now the WSF is threatened by its own success. The safe, open, festive atmosphere of the forum has allowed politicians and nongovernmental organizations that are imbricated in the political and economic systems that the forum opposes to participate and make themselves heard.

Another danger is that the WSF, which has played such a vital role in the movement for global justice, runs the risk of becoming an end unto itself. Just organizing it every year consumes the energies of some of the best activists. If *conversations* about resistance replace real civil disobedience, then the WSF could become an asset to those whom it was created to oppose. The forum must be held and must grow, but we have to find ways to channel our conversations there back into concrete action.

As resistance movements have begun to reach out across national borders and pose a real threat, governments have developed their own strategies of how to deal with them. They range from cooptation to repression.

I'm going to speak about three of the contemporary dangers that confront resistance movements: the difficult meeting point between mass movements and the mass media, the hazards of the NGO-ization of resistance, and the confrontation between resistance movements and increasingly repressive states.

The place in which the mass media meets mass movements is a complicated one.

Governments have learned that a crisis-driven media cannot afford to hang about in the same place for too long. Like a business needs cash turnover, the media need crises turnover. Whole countries become old news. They cease to exist, and the darkness becomes deeper than before the light was briefly shone on them. We saw it happen in Afghanistan when the Soviets withdrew. And now, after Operation Enduring Freedom put the CIA's Hamid Karzai in place, Afghanistan has been thrown to its warlords once more. Another CIA operative, Iyad Allawi, has been installed in Iraq, so perhaps it's time for the media to move on from there, too.

While governments hone the art of waiting out crises, resistance movements are increasingly being ensnared in a vortex of crisis production, seeking to find ways of manufacturing them in easily consumable, spectator-friendly formats. Every self-respecting people's movement, every "issue," is expected to have its own hot air balloon in the sky advertising its brand and purpose. For this reason, starvation deaths are more effective advertisements for impov-

37

erishment than millions of malnourished people, who don't quite make the cut. Dams are not newsworthy until the devastation they wreak makes good television. (And by then, it's too late.)

Standing in the rising water of a reservoir for days on end, watching your home and belongings float away to protest against a big dam used to be an effective strategy, but isn't any more. The media is dead bored of that one. So the hundreds of thousands of people being displaced by dams are expected to either conjure new tricks or give up the struggle.

Resistance as spectacle, as political theater, has a history. Gandhi's salt march in 1931 to Dandi is among the most exhilarating examples. But the salt march wasn't theater alone. It was the symbolic part of a larger act of real civil disobedience. When Gandhi and an army of freedom fighters marched to Gujarat's coast and made salt from seawater, thousands of Indians across the country began to make their own salt, openly defying imperial Britain's salt tax laws, which banned local salt production in favor of British salt imports. It was a direct strike at the economic underpinning of the British Empire.

The disturbing thing nowadays is that resistance as spectacle has cut loose from its origins in genuine civil disobedience and is beginning to become more symbolic than real. Colorful demonstrations and weekend marches are vital but alone are not powerful enough to stop wars. Wars will be stopped only when soldiers refuse to fight, when workers refuse to load weapons onto ships and aircraft, when people boycott the economic outposts of Empire that are strung across the globe.

If we want to reclaim the space for civil disobedience, we will have to liberate ourselves from the tyranny of crisis reportage and its fear of the mundane. We have to use our experience, our imagination, and our art to interrogate those instruments of state that ensure that "normality" remains what it is: cruel, unjust, unacceptable. We have to expose the policies and processes that make ordinary things—food, water, shelter and dignity—such a distant dream for ordinary people. The real pre-emptive strike is to understand that wars are the end result of a flawed and unjust peace.

As far as mass resistance movements are concerned, the fact is that no amount of media coverage can make up for mass strength on the ground. There is no option, really, to old-fashioned, back-breaking political mobilization. Corporate globalization has increased the distance between those who make decisions and those who have to suffer the effects of those decisions. Forums like the WSF enable local resistance movements to reduce that distance and to link up with their counterparts in rich countries. That alliance is a formidable one. For example, when India's first private dam, the Maheshwar Dam, was being built, alliances between the Narmada Bachao Andolan (NBA), the German organization Urgewald, the Berne Declaration in Switzerland, and the

International Rivers Network in Berkeley worked together to push a series of international banks and corporations out of the project. This would not have been possible had there not been a rock solid resistance movement on the ground. The voice of that local movement was amplified by supporters on the global stage, embarrassing investors and forcing them to withdraw.

An infinite number of similar alliances, targeting specific projects and specific corporations would help to make another world possible. We should begin with the corporations who did business with Saddam Hussein and now profit from the devastation and occupation of Iraq.

A second hazard facing mass movements is the NGO-ization of resistance. It will be easy to twist what I'm about to say into an indictment of all NGOs. That would be a falsehood. In the murky waters of fake NGOs set up to siphon off grant money or as tax dodges (in states like Bihar, they are given as dowry), of course there are NGOs doing valuable work. But it's important to turn our attention away from the positive work being done by some individual NGOs, and consider the NGO phenomenon in a broader political context.

In India, for instance, the funded NGO boom began in the late 1980s and 1990s. It coincided with the opening of India's markets to neoliberalism. At the time, the Indian state, in keeping with the requirements of structural adjustment, was withdrawing funding from rural development, agriculture, energy, transport, and public health. As the state abdicated its traditional role, NGOs moved in to work in these very areas. The difference, of course, is that the funds available to them are a minuscule fraction of the actual cut in public spending. Most large well-funded NGOs are financed and patronized by aid and development agencies, which are in turn funded by Western governments, the World Bank, the UN, and some multinational corporations. Though they may not be the very same agencies, they are certainly part of the same loose, political formation that oversees the neoliberal project and demands the slash in government spending in the first place.

Why should these agencies fund NGOs? Could it be just old-fashioned missionary zeal? Guilt? It's a little more than that.

NGOs give the *impression* that they are filling the vacuum created by a retreating state. And they are, but in a materially inconsequential way. Their *real* contribution is that they defuse political anger and dole out as aid or benevolence what people ought to have by right. They alter the public psyche. They turn people into dependent victims and blunt the edges of political resistance. NGOs form a sort of buffer between the *sarkar* and *public*. Between Empire and its subjects. They have become the arbitrators, the interpreters, the facilitators of the discourse. They play out the role of the "reasonable man" in an unfair, unreasonable war.

In the long run, NGOs are accountable to their funders, not to the people they work among. They're what botanists would call an indicator species. It's almost as though the greater the devastation caused by neoliberalism, the greater the outbreak of NGOs. Nothing illustrates this more poignantly than the phenomenon of the U.S. preparing to invade a country and simultaneously readying NGOs to go in and clean up the devastation.

In order to make sure their funding is not jeopardized and that the governments of the countries they work in will allow them to function, NGOs have to present their work—whether it's in a country devastated by war, poverty or an epidemic of disease—within a shallow framework more or less shorn of a political or historical context. At any rate, an *inconvenient* historical or political context. It's not for nothing that the "NGO perspective" is becoming increasingly respected.

Apolitical (and therefore, actually, extremely

political) distress reports from poor countries and war zones eventually make the (dark) people of those (dark) countries seem like pathological victims. *Another malnourished Indian, another starving Ethiopian, another Afghan refugee camp, another maimed Sudanese* . . . in need of the white man's help. They unwittingly reinforce racist stereotypes and re-affirm the achievements, the comforts, and the compassion (the tough love) of Western civilization, minus the guilt of the history of genocide, colonialism, and slavery. They're the secular missionaries of the modern world.

Eventually—on a smaller scale, but more insidiously—the capital available to NGOs plays the same role in alternative politics as the speculative capital that flows in and out of the economies of poor countries. It begins to dictate the agenda.

It turns confrontation into negotiation. It depoliticizes resistance. It interferes with local peoples' movements that have traditionally been self-reliant. NGOs have funds that can employ local people who might otherwise be activists in resistance movements, but now can feel they are doing some immediate, creative good (and earning a living while they're at it). Charity offers instant gratification to the giver, as well as the receiver, but its side effects can be dangerous. Real political resistance offers no such short cuts.

The NGO-ization of politics threatens to turn resistance into a well-mannered, reasonable, salaried, 9-to-5 job. With a few perks thrown in.

Real resistance has real consequences. And no salary.

This brings us to a third danger I want to speak about tonight: the deadly nature of the actual confrontation between resistance movements and increasingly repressive states. Between public power and the agents of Empire.

Whenever civil resistance has shown the slightest signs of evolving from symbolic action into anything remotely threatening, the crackdown is merciless. We've seen what happened in the demonstrations in Seattle, in Miami, in Gothenburg, in Genoa.

In the United States, you have the USA PATRIOT Act, which has become a blueprint for antiterrorism laws passed by governments around the world. Freedoms are being curbed in the name of protecting freedom. And once we surrender our freedoms, to win them back will take a revolution.

Some governments have vast experience in the business of curbing freedoms and still smelling sweet. The government of India, an old hand at the game, lights the path. Over the years the Indian government has passed a plethora of laws that allow it to call almost anyone a terrorist, an insurgent, a militant. We have the Armed Forces Special Powers Act, the Public Security Act, the Special Areas Security Act, the Gangster Act, the Terrorist and Disruptive Areas Act (which has formally lapsed, but under which people are still facing trial), and, most recently, POTA (the Prevention of Terrorism Act), the broad-spectrum antibiotic for the disease of dissent.

There are other steps that are being taken, such as court judgments that in effect curtail free speech, the right of government workers to go on strike, the right to life and livelihood. Courts have begun to micro-manage our lives in India. And criticizing the courts is a criminal offense.

But coming back to the counterterrorism initiatives, over the last decade the number of people who have been killed by the police and security forces runs into the tens of thousands. In the state of Andhra Pradesh (the pin-up girl of corporate globalization in India), an average of about 200 "extremists" are killed in what are called "encounters" every year. The Bombay police boast of how many "gangsters" they have killed in "shoot outs." In Kashmir, in a situation that almost amounts to war, an estimated 80,000 people have been killed since 1989. Thousands have simply "disappeared." In the northeastern provinces, the situation is similar.

In recent years, the Indian police have opened fire on unarmed people at peaceful demonstrations, mostly Dalit and Adivasi. The preferred method is to kill them and then call them terrorists. India is not alone, though. We have seen similar things happen in countries such Bolivia and Chile. In the era of neoliberalism, poverty is a crime and protesting against it is more and more being defined as terrorism.

In India, the Prevention of Terrorism Act (POTA) is often called the *Production* of Terrorism Act. It's a versatile, hold-all law that could apply to anyone from an al-Qaeda operative to a disgruntled bus conductor. As with all antiterrorism laws, the genius of POTA is that it can be whatever the government wants. For example, in Tamil Nadu, it has been used to imprison and silence critics of the state government. In Jharkhand 3,200 people, mostly poor Adivasis accused of being Maoists, have been named in criminal complaints under POTA. In Gujarat and Mumbai, the Act is used almost exclusively against Muslims. After the 2002 state-assisted pogrom in Gujarat, in which an estimated 2,000 Muslims were savagely killed by Hindu mobs and 150,000 driven from their homes, 287 people have been accused under POTA. Of these, 286 are Muslim and *one* is a Sikh.

POTA allows confessions extracted in police custody to be admitted as judicial evidence. In effect, torture tends to replace investigation. The South Asia Human Rights Documentation Center reports that India has the highest number of torture and custodial deaths in the world. Government records show that there were 1,307 deaths in judicial custody in 2002 alone.

A few months ago, I was a member of a peoples' tribunal on POTA. Over a period of two days, we listened to harrowing testimonies of what is happening in our wonderful democracy. It's everything—from people being forced to drink urine, being stripped, humiliated, given electric shocks, burned with cigarette butts, having iron rods put up their anuses, to people being beaten and kicked to death.

The new government has promised to repeal POTA. I'd be surprised if that happens before similar legislation under a different name is put in place.

When every avenue of nonviolent dissent is closed down, and everyone who protests against the violation of their human rights is called a terrorist, should we really be surprised if vast parts of the country are overrun by those who believe in armed struggle and are more or less beyond the control of the state: in Kashmir, the northeastern provinces, large parts of Madhya Pradesh, Chattisgarh, Jharkhand, and Andhra Pradesh. Ordinary people in these regions are trapped between the violence of the militants and the state.

In Kashmir, the Indian army estimates that 3,000 to 4,000 militants are operating at any given time. To control them, the Indian government deploys about 500,000 soldiers. Clearly, it isn't just the militants the army seeks to control, but a whole population of humiliated, unhappy people who see the Indian army as an occupation force. The primary purpose of laws like POTA is not to target real terrorists or militants, who are usually simply shot. Anti-terrorism laws are used to intimidate civil society. Inevitably, such repression has the effect of fueling discontent and anger.

The Armed Forces Special Powers Act allows not just officers, but even junior commissioned officers and non-commissioned officers of the army, to use force and even kill any person on *suspicion* of disturbing public order. It was first imposed on a few districts in the state of Manipur in 1958. Today, it applies to virtually all of the northeast and Kashmir. The documentation of instances of torture, disappearances, custodial deaths, rape, and summary execution by security forces is enough to turn your stomach.

In Andhra Pradesh, in India's heartland, the militant Marxist Leninist Peoples' War Group—which for years has been engaged in a violent armed struggle and has been the principal target of many of the Andhra police's fake "encounters"—held its first public meeting in years on July 28, 2004, in the town of Warangal.

The former chief minister of Andhra Pradesh, Chandrababu Naidu, liked to call himself the CEO of the state. In return for his enthusiasm in implementing structural adjustment, Andhra Pradesh received millions of dollars of aid from the World Bank and development agencies such as Britain's Department for International Development. As a result of structural adjustment, Andhra Pradesh is now best known for two things: the hundreds of suicides by farmers who were steeped in debt and the spreading influence and growing militancy of the Peoples' War Group. During Naidu's term in office, the PWG were not arrested, or captured, they were summarily shot.

In response, the PWG campaigned actively, and let it be said, violently, against Naidu. In May, the Congress won the state elections. The Naidu government didn't just lose, it was humiliated in the polls. When the PWG called a public meeting, it was attended by hundreds of thousands of people. Under POTA, all of them are considered terrorists. Are they all going to be detained in some Indian equivalent of Guantánamo Bay? The whole of the northeast and the Kashmir valley is in ferment. What will the government do with these millions of people?

One does not endorse the violence of these militant groups. Neither morally nor strategically. But to condemn it without first denouncing the much greater violence perpetrated by the state would be to deny the people of these regions not just their basic human rights, but even the right to a fair hearing. People who have lived in situations of conflict are in no doubt that militancy and armed struggle provokes a massive escalation of violence from the state. But living as they do, in situations of unbearable injustice, can they remain silent forever?

There is no discussion taking place in the world today that is more crucial than the debate about strategies of resistance. And the choice of strategy is not entirely in the hands of the *public*. It is also in the hands of *sarkar*.

After all, when the U.S. invades and occupies Iraq in the way it has done, with such overwhelming military force, can the resistance be expected to be a conventional military one? (Of course, even if it *were* conventional, it would still be called terrorist.) In a strange sense, the U.S. government's arsenal of weapons and unrivalled air and fire power makes terrorism an all-but-inescapable response. What people lack in wealth and power, they will make up for with stealth and strategy.

In the twenty-first century, the connection between corporate globalization, religious fundamentalism, nuclear nationalism, and the pauperization of whole populations is becoming impossible to ignore. The unrest has myriad manifestations: terrorism, armed struggle, nonviolent mass resistance, and common crime.

In this restive, despairing time, if governments do not do all they can to honor nonviolent resistance, then by default they privilege those who turn to violence. No government's condemnation of terrorism is credible if it cannot show itself to be open to change by nonviolent dissent. But instead nonviolent resistance movements are being crushed. Any kind of mass political mobilization or organization is being bought off, broken, or simply ignored.

Meanwhile, governments and the corporate media, and let's not forget the film industry, lavish their time, attention, funds, technology, research, and admiration on war and terrorism. Violence has been deified. The message this sends is disturbing and dangerous: If you seek to air a public grievance, violence is more effective than nonviolence.

As the rift between the rich and poor grows, as the need to appropriate and control the world's resources to feed the great capitalist machine becomes more urgent, the unrest will only escalate.

For those of us who are on the wrong side of Empire, the humiliation is becoming unbearable. Each of the Iraqi children killed by the United States was our child. Each of the prisoners tortured in Abu Ghraib was our comrade. Each of their screams was ours. When they were humiliated, we were humiliated.

The U.S. soldiers fighting in Iraq—mostly volunteers in a poverty draft from small towns and poor urban neighborhoods—are victims, just as much as the Iraqis, of the same horrendous process, which asks them to die for a victory that will never be theirs.

The mandarins of the corporate world, the CEOs, the bankers, the politicians, the judges and generals look down on us from on high and shake their heads sternly. "There's no alternative," they say, and let slip the dogs of war.

Then, from the ruins of Afghanistan, from the rubble of Iraq and Chechnya, from the streets of occupied Palestine and the mountains of Kashmir, from the hills and plains of Colombia, and the forests of Andhra Pradesh and Assam, comes the chilling reply: "There's no alternative but terrorism." Terrorism. Armed struggle. Insurgency. Call it what you want.

Terrorism is vicious, ugly, and dehumanizing for its perpetrators as well as its victims. But so is war. You could say that terrorism is the privatization of war. Terrorists are the free marketers of war. They are people who don't believe that the state has a monopoly on the legitimate use of violence.

Human society is journeying to a terrible place.

Of course, there is an alternative to terrorism. It's called justice.

It's time to recognize that no amount of nuclear weapons, or full spectrum dominance, or "daisy cutters," or spurious governing councils and loya jirgas, can buy peace at the cost of justice.

The urge for hegemony and preponderance by some will be matched with greater intensity by the longing for dignity and justice by others.

Exactly what form that battle takes, whether it's beautiful or bloodthirsty, depends on us.

ABOUT THE AUTHOR

ARUNDHATI ROY is the author of the novel, *The God of Small Things*, for which she was awarded the Booker Prize in 1997. She has also published four essay collections: *An Ordinary Person's Guide to Empire*, *War Talk*, *Power Politics*, and *The Cost of Living*, and is the subject of *The Checkbook and the Cruise Missile: Interviews with Arundhati Roy*, edited by David Barsamian. Roy received the 2002 Lannan Award for Cultural Freedom from the Lannan Foundation. Trained as an architect, Roy lives in New Delhi, India.

ABOUT THE TEXT

The text of *Public Power in the Age of Empire* is based on a public address that Arundhati Roy delivered to an overflow crowd at the American Sociological Association's 99th Annual Meeting in San Francisco, California, on August 16, 2004. The theme of the conference was "Public Sociologies."

The talk quickly aired on C-SPAN *Book TV*, *Democracy Now!*, and *Alternative Radio*, reaching audiences throughout North America and beyond, and was circulated via e-mail around the world.

OTHER OPEN MEDIA TITLES

9-11
by Noam Chomsky

America's Disappeared
edited by Rachel Meeropol

Are Prisons Obsolete?
by Angela Davis

Artists in Times of War
by Howard Zinn

The Battle for Saudi Arabia
by As`ad AbuKhalil

Iraq, Inc.
by Pratap Chatterjee

Israel/Palestine
by Tanya Reinhart

Media Control
by Noam Chomsky

North Korea/South Korea
by John Feffer

Our Media, Not Theirs
by Robert W. McChesney and John Nichols

Sent by Earth
by Alice Walker

Silencing Political Dissent
by Nancy Chang

Terrorism and War
by Howard Zinn with Anthony Arnove

Terrorism, Theirs & Ours
by Eqbal Ahmad with David Barsamian

To order call 1-800-596-7437,
or visit www.sevenstories.com